GIFT WISHES

Grace - Full Gift Baskets
197 Crestwood St.
Troutdale, OR 97060
(503) 618-8818

by Barbara Deede

© 1992 by Barbara Deede
Seattle, Washington

Design by Colleen Whitten Srull

All rights reserved. No part of this book may be reproduced in any form by any means, without the written permission from the publisher.

ISBN 0-9627619-1-5

Published by Deede Press
4545 Sandpoint Way Northeast
Seattle, WA 98105

INTRODUCTION

This book was conceived out of my own need to make gift giving the pleasurable experience it is supposed to be. I wanted to end the frustration of shopping with only a vague notion of someone's gift wishes and to eliminate the disappointment of receiving the well-meant but unsuitable present.

We all need suggestions and reminders. For instance, I have a loving husband, Daryl, who simply can't remember which chocolates I adore, and I can't remember my family's sizes, or stay in touch with the latest teenage fad. Our family needed the Gift Wish book to record ideas in advance and to consult later when planning gift selections. So this book was born.

Now, my "Gift Wish" for you is for this book to help you and your family carefully plan your gift buying for all those wonderful occasions throughout the year.

Barbara

CONTENTS

Family Gift Wishes

Friends' Gift Wishes

Books – Subject, Title & Author

Apparel – Size & Color

Food & Wine

Gifts Given

Gifts Received

Special Dates to Remember

Family Gift Wishes

Family Gift Wishes

Name

Wishes

Family Gift Wishes

Name

Wishes

Family Gift Wishes

Name

Wishes

Family Gift Wishes

Name

Wishes

Family Gift Wishes

Name

Wishes

Family Gift Wishes

Name

Wishes

Family Gift Wishes

Name

Wishes

Family Gift Wishes

Name

Wishes

Family Gift Wishes

Name

Wishes

Family Gift Wishes

Name

Wishes

Family Gift Wishes

Name

Wishes

Family Gift Wishes

Name

Wishes

Family Gift Wishes

Name

Wishes

Family Gift Wishes

Name

Wishes

Family Gift Wishes

Name

Wishes

Family Gift Wishes

Name

Wishes

Family Gift Wishes

Name

Wishes

Family Gift Wishes

Name

Wishes

Family Gift Wishes

Name

Wishes

FAMILY GIFT WISHES

Name

Wishes

Family Gift Wishes

Name

Wishes

Family Gift Wishes

Name

Wishes

FAMILY GIFT WISHES

Name

Wishes

Family Gift Wishes

Name

Wishes

FAMILY GIFT WISHES

Name

Wishes

Family Gift Wishes

Name

Wishes

Family Gift Wishes

Name

Wishes

Family Gift Wishes

Name

Wishes

FAMILY GIFT WISHES

Name

Wishes

Family Gift Wishes

Name

Wishes

Family Gift Wishes

Name

Wishes

Family Gift Wishes

Name

Wishes

Family Gift Wishes

Name

Wishes

Family Gift Wishes

Name

Wishes

Family Gift Wishes

Name

Wishes

Family Gift Wishes

Name

Wishes

Family Gift Wishes

Name

Wishes

Friends' Gift Wishes

Friends' Gift Wishes

Name

Wishes

Friends' Gift Wishes

Name

Wishes

Friends' Gift Wishes

Name

Wishes

Friends' Gift Wishes

Name

Wishes

Friends' Gift Wishes

Name

Wishes

Friends' Gift Wishes

Name

Wishes

Friends' Gift Wishes

Name

Wishes

Friends' Gift Wishes

Name

Wishes

Friends' Gift Wishes

Name

Wishes

BOOKS

Books

| Name | Title & Author | Subject |

Books

Name   *Title & Author*   *Subject*

Books

Name   *Title & Author*   *Subject*

Books

Name   *Title & Author*   *Subject*

Books

Name	Title & Author	Subject

Books

Name	Title & Author	Subject

Books

Name   *Title & Author*   *Subject*

Apparel

Apparel

Name   *Size & Color*

APPAREL

Name *Size & Color*

Apparel

Name   *Size & Color*

Apparel

Name   *Size & Color*

Apparel

Name *Size & Color*

Apparel

Name   *Size & Color*

Apparel

Name   *Size & Color*

Food & Wine

Food & Wine

Food & Wine

Food & Wine

Food & Wine

Food & Wine

Food & Wine

Food & Wine

GIFTS GIVEN

Gifts Given

Name *Date*

Gifts Given

Name *Date*

GIFTS GIVEN

Name *Date*

Gifts Given

Name *Date*

GIFTS GIVEN

Name *Date*

Gifts Given

Name   Date

Gifts Given

Name *Date*

Gifts Received

Gifts Received

Name   *Date*   *Thank-you sent*

Gifts Received

Name   Date   Thank-you sent

Gifts Received

Name　　　　　　　　*Date*　　　　　　　　*Thank-you sent*

Gifts Received

Name	Date	Thank-you sent

Gifts Received

Name	Date	Thank-you sent

Gifts Received

Name *Date* *Thank-you sent*

GIFTS RECEIVED

Name *Date* *Thank-you sent*

Special Dates *to* Remember

January

	1	2	3	4	5	6	7
	8	9	10	11	12	13	14
	15	16	17	18	19	20	21
	22	23	24	25	26	27	28
	29	30	31				

Notes

FEBRUARY

1	2	3	4	5	6	7
8	9	10	11	12	13	14
15	16	17	18	19	20	21
22	23	24	25	26	27	28
29						

Notes

MARCH

1	2	3	4	5	6	7
8	9	10	11	12	13	14
15	16	17	18	19	20	21
22	23	24	25	26	27	28
29	30	31				

Notes

APRIL

1	2	3
8	9	10
15	16	17
22	23	24
29	30	

4	5	6	7
11	12	13	14
18	19	20	21
25	26	27	28

Notes

MAY

1	2	3	4	5	6	7
8	9	10	11	12	13	14
15	16	17	18	19	20	21
22	23	24	25	26	27	28
29	30	31				

Notes

JUNE

1	8	15	22	29
2	9	16	23	30
3	10	17	24	
4	11	18	25	
5	12	19	26	
6	13	20	27	
7	14	21	28	

Notes

JULY

1	2	3	4	5	6	7
8	9	10	11	12	13	14
15	16	17	18	19	20	21
22	23	24	25	26	27	28
29	30	31				

Notes

AUGUST

1	8	15	22	29
2	9	16	23	30
3	10	17	24	31
4	11	18	25	
5	12	19	26	
6	13	20	27	
7	14	21	28	

Notes

SEPTEMBER

1	2	3	4	5	6	7
8	9	10	11	12	13	14
15	16	17	18	19	20	21
22	23	24	25	26	27	28
29	30					

Notes

OCTOBER

1	2	3	4	5	6	7
8	9	10	11	12	13	14
15	16	17	18	19	20	21
22	23	24	25	26	27	28
29	30	31				

Notes

NOVEMBER

1	2	3	4	5	6	7
8	9	10	11	12	13	14
15	16	17	18	19	20	21
22	23	24	25	26	27	28
29	30					

Notes

December

1	2	3	4	5	6	7
8	9	10	11	12	13	14
15	16	17	18	19	20	21
22	23	24	25	26	27	28
29	30	31				

Notes